This dragon book belongs to:

....

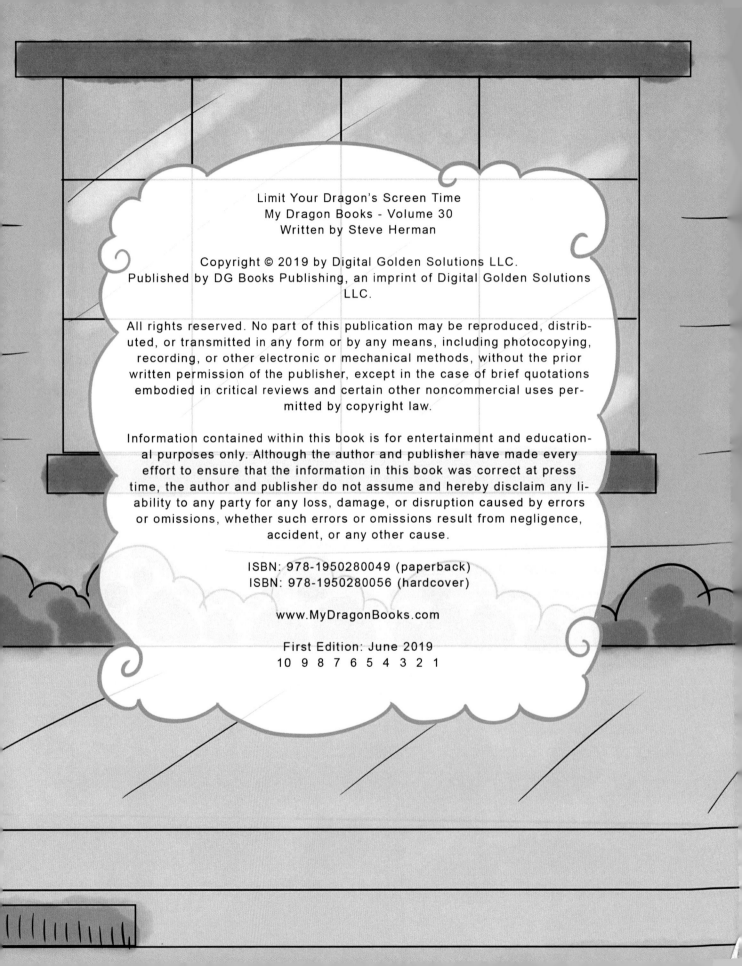

Limit Your Dragon's Screen Time
My Dragon Books - Volume 30
Written by Steve Herman

ISBN: 978-1950280049 (paperback)
ISBN: 978-1950280056 (hardcover)

www.MyDragonBooks.com

First Edition: June 2019
10 9 8 7 6 5 4 3 2 1

Limit Your Dragon's Screen Time

My Dragon Books - Volume 30

Steve Herman

Hi, I'm Drew. Remember me?
I'm not too easy to forget -
I'm the kid with Diggory Doo,
a real live dragon for a pet.

We have written lots of books –
Perhaps you've read these books before –
Diggory needed lots of training –
Are you ready for one more?

I've taught Diggory manners and proper things that he should do, How not to lose his temper, and I've potty-trained him, too!

But there was still another thing
I could clearly see
That Diggory needed to learn –
Let's see if you agree.

Although he wasn't naughty,
and he wasn't acting mean,
It always seemed that
Diggory was looking at a screen!

Whenever I would talk to him, Diggory wouldn't hear, Since he was watching videos with an earbud in his ear.

When he was playing games, he would never want to quit, And if I tried to make him, he might even throw a fit.

He watched videos when walking,
and would often trip and fall,

Or not see where he was going
and would walk into a wall!

When it was time to go to sleep, he took his phone to bed;

He put it on the dinner table right beside the bread!

He took it on the school bus, to the park, and to the mall;

He even took his phone right into the bathroom stall!

He got caught watching videos
and playing games at school,
Even though Diggory knew
that he was breaking teacher's rule;

BORING.

When Diggory Doo got bored,
instead of trying something new,
He'd play a game, or text,
or scroll through videos to view.

Diggory Doo played games so much,
he thought that they were real!
He was simply stuck in his virtual world,
and how it made him feel.

"Diggory Doo!" I scolded,
"You must surely realize...
That this addiction has to stop!"
but Diggory rolled his eyes.

We turned off all technology
and stored it on a shelf,
So he could hang with others
and not be by himself.

Since he no longer had devices
to keep him company,
We decided he should start the week
by spending time with *me*.

The first day, we cooked dinner –
Mom and Dad were very proud –
– Diggory Doo obeyed the rule –
"No devices are allowed!"

We talked together as we worked.
I said, "It's been a while
Since we've hung out in the kitchen,"
and that made Diggory smile.

Day two was spent in climbing trees and riding on our bikes,

And other fun activities I knew that Diggory liked.

Diggory had forgotten that he loved being outdoors – Soon Diggory Doo declared, "I kind of like this plan of yours!"

Day three we focused mostly on some healthy things to do Like exercise and walking and a game of tennis, too.

Day five we read some books –
Diggory admitted, "That was fun!"

"Before the raindrops kiss your cheeks,
you smell them on the breeze,
And don't you love the sweet perfume
that drips from jasmine trees?"

"Then take a whiff of fresh cut grass –
You can almost smell the *green*.
A nose is quite amazing,
when it's not buried in a screen."

At first my dragon had his doubts, but Diggory Doo agreed
That though devices could be fun, he didn't really need...

To fill the hours of every day
by looking at a screen –
"That's pretty lame!" said Diggory Doo,
"if you know what I mean!"

Diggory still likes videos
and will play a game or two,
But too much isn't healthy,
and he has better things to do,

There's stuff he doesn't want to miss,
and the place he wants to be...
Is living in the *real world*
and not fake technology!

Read more about Drew and Diggory Doo!

TEACH YOUR DRAGON TO SHARE
Steve Herman

FIX YOUR DRAGON'S ATTITUDE
Steve Herman

GET YOUR DRAGON TO TRY NEW THINGS
Steve Herman

TEACH YOUR DRAGON TO FOLLOW INSTRUCTIONS
Steve Herman

HELP YOUR DRAGON DEAL WITH ANXIETY
Steve Herman

A DRAGON CHRISTMAS
Steve Herman

TEACH YOUR DRAGON MANNERS
Steve Herman

TEACH YOUR DRAGON EMPATHY
Steve Herman

TEACH YOUR DRAGON About DIVERSITY
Steve Herman

HELP YOUR DRAGON Learn From MISTAKES
Steve Herman

HELP YOUR DRAGON DEAL WITH CHANGE
Steve Herman

THE SAD DRAGON
A DRAGON BOOK ABOUT GRIEF AND LOSS
Steve Herman

DRAGON SIBLING RIVALRY
Steve Herman

LIMIT YOUR DRAGON'S SCREEN TIME
Steve Herman

Visit
www.MyDragonBooks.com
for more!

Made in the USA
Middletown, DE
06 August 2020

14640816R00027